SPIRITUAL YOGA

Other Works by the Author

Bhagavad-gītā As It Is

Śrīmad-Bhāgavatam

Śrī Caitanya-caritāmṛta

Kṛṣṇa, the Supreme Personality of Godhead

Teachings of Lord Caitanya

The Nectar of Devotion

The Nectar of Instruction

Śrī Īśopaniṣad

Light of the Bhāgavata

Easy Journey to Other Planets

Teachings of Lord Kapila, the Son of Devahūti

Teachings of Queen Kuntī

The Science of Self-Realization

SPIRITUAL YOGA

Living a Life Inspired by Love

His Divine Grace
A. C. Bhaktivedanta Swami Prabhupāda
Founder-*Ācārya* of the International Society for Krishna Consciousness

THE BHAKTIVEDANTA BOOK TRUST

Readers interested in the subject matter of this book are invited by the International Society for Krishna Consciousness (ISKCON) to visit or contact any of its centers. Please refer to the address list at the back of the book.

To order books published by
The Bhaktivedanta Book Trust,
go to blservices.com

bbt.se
bbtmedia.com
bbt.org
krishna.com
krishna.se

ISBN 978-91-7769-454-0

Printed in 2024
EN-SY-2024-TEXT-R15

Contents

Introduction

There's yoga for the body and yoga for the soul. This book is about yoga for the soul: *bhakti-yoga,* or the yoga of the highest pleasure, of pure love and devotion.

Most people are familiar with yoga for the body, but yoga purely for the soul is new to most people. You won't find it portrayed on the covers of books and magazines; it's practiced at the soul level. In the type of yoga you practice for your physical and mental well-being, you stretch your mind and body and feel energized for a while. Stretching your soul's "muscles" and finding out who you are at your innermost core is something different altogether. If you're successful at it, it will leave you feeling energized forever.

This book will introduce you to some of the aspects of *bhakti-yoga* and teach you how to add its practices into your daily life. If you're ready for the *ultimate* yoga practice, the spiritual yoga of the soul awaits you.

Bhakti-yoga is nothing new. Long before the first teachers of yoga asanas ever opened a studio in the West, teachers of spiritual yoga were sitting on mountaintops and in forests in ancient India teaching their students the secrets to attaining the highest pleasure.

For those who really know, attaining this pleasure of the soul is the highest goal. But to achieve it, you have to know the path. And you can find that out only from one who knows it, a teacher of *bhakti-yoga*.

One of these teachers is described in this book. His name is Śrī Ṛṣabhadeva, an incarnation of the Divine who lived millions of years ago, according to Vedic texts. Externally, he served as a great king, which means he had the chance to enjoy every kind of material pleasure. But to set the perfect example of self-control, he instead emphasized sense restraint and focus on self-realization. Before retiring his kingship, he taught the techniques of spiritual yoga to his sons.

For centuries afterward, this knowledge was disseminated orally, held in the memories of sages and passed from spiritual master to disciple. As time passed and people's power of memory began to decline, the great compiler of the *Vedas* named Vyāsa put Ṛṣabhadeva's teachings into writing and included them in his opus, the *Śrīmad-Bhāgavatam*. Even so, for a long time afterward, only a chosen few in India learned these teachings.

Then, in the late twentieth century, His Divine Grace A.C. Bhaktivedanta Swami Prabhupāda, the greatest spiritual master of the modern age, following the orders of his own spiritual master, translated Ṛṣabhadeva's teachings on spiritual yoga into English and brought them to the Western world, giving you the chance to step onto the path that will lead you to the highest pleasure.

This book is a combination of Śrīla Prabhupāda's published translation and commentary on the original

Sanskrit teachings of Ṛṣabhadeva, as they were recorded in *Śrīmad-Bhāgavatam* 5.5.1–14, and the transcripts of a series of lectures Śrīla Prabhupāda gave on these same teachings in London, Stockholm, and Vṛndāvana, India, between 1969 and 1976.

We hope you find benefit in these teachings and that they help you in every way possible to find the highest pleasure.

The Editors

Chapter One

Don't Be Like Hogs and Dogs

ṛṣabha uvāca
nāyaṁ deho deha-bhājāṁ nṛloke
kaṣṭān kāmān arhate viḍ-bhujāṁ ye
tapo divyaṁ putrakā yena sattvaṁ
śuddhyed yasmād brahma-
saukhyaṁ tv anantam

"Lord Ṛṣabhadeva told His sons: 'My dear boys, of all the living entities who have accepted material bodies in this world, one who has been awarded this human form should not work hard day and night simply for sense gratification, which is available even for dogs and for hogs that eat stool. One should engage in penance and austerity to attain the divine position of devotional service. By such activity, one's heart is purified, and when one attains this position, he attains eternal, blissful life, which is transcendental to material happiness and which continues forever.'"

Śrīmad-Bhāgavatam 5.5.1

In this verse Lord Ṛṣabhadeva tells His sons about the importance of human life. The word *deha-bhāk* refers to anyone who accepts a material body, but the living entity who is awarded the human form must act differently from animals. Animals like dogs and hogs enjoy sense gratification by eating stool. After undergoing severe hardships all day, human beings are trying to enjoy themselves at night by eating, drinking, having sex, and sleeping. At the same time, they have to properly defend themselves. However, this is not human civilization. Human life means voluntarily practicing suffering for the advancement of spiritual life. There is, of course, suffering in the lives of animals and plants, which are suffering due to their past misdeeds. However, human beings should voluntarily accept suffering in the form of austerities and penances in order to attain the divine life. After attaining the divine life, one can enjoy happiness eternally. After all, every living entity is trying to enjoy happiness, but as long as one is encaged in the material body he has to suffer different kinds of misery. A higher sense is present in the human form. We should act according to superior advice in order to attain eternal happiness and go back to Godhead.

It is significant in this verse that the government and the natural guardian, the father, should educate subordinates and raise them to Kṛṣṇa consciousness. Devoid of Kṛṣṇa consciousness, every living being suffers in this cycle of birth and death perpetually. To relieve them from this bondage and enable them to become blissful and happy, *bhakti-yoga* should be taught. A foolish civilization neglects to teach people how to rise to the platform of *bhakti-yoga*. Without Kṛṣṇa consciousness a person is no better than a hog or dog. The instructions of Ṛṣabhadeva are very essential at the present moment. People are being educated and trained to work very hard for sense gratification, and there is no sublime aim in life. A man travels to earn his livelihood, leaving home early in the morning, catching a local train, and being packed in a compartment. He has to stand for an hour or two in order to reach his place of business. Then again he takes a bus to get to the office. At the office he works hard from nine to five; then he takes two or three hours to return home. After eating, he has sex and goes to sleep. For all this hardship, his only happiness is a little sex. *Yan maithunādi-gṛhamedhi-sukhaṁ hi tuccham*. Ṛṣabhadeva clearly states that human life is not meant for this kind of existence, which is enjoyed even by dogs and hogs. Indeed, dogs and hogs do not have to work so hard for sex. A human being should try to live in a different way and should not try to imitate dogs and hogs. The alternative is mentioned. Human life is meant for *tapasya,* austerity and penance. By *tapasya,* one can get out of the material clutches. When one is situated in Kṛṣṇa consciousness, devotional service, his happiness is guaranteed eternally. By taking to *bhakti-yoga,* devotional service, one's existence is purified. The living entity is seeking happiness life after life, but he can make a solution to all his problems simply by practicing *bhakti-yoga*. Then he immediately becomes eligible to return home, back to Godhead. As confirmed in the *Bhagavad-gītā* (4.9):

janma karma ca me divyam
evaṁ yo vetti tattvataḥ
tyaktvā dehaṁ punar janma
naiti mām eti so 'rjuna

"One who knows the transcendental nature of My appearance and activities does not, upon leaving the body, take his birth again in this material world, but attains My eternal abode, O Arjuna."

Now the question might be, "What is the meaning of *tapasya* – austerities and penances?" *Tapasya* means voluntarily agreeing to mold your life according to the rules and regulations given by the scriptures, the spiritual master, and the saintly persons. So Lord Ṛṣabhadeva is instructing His sons, "My dear sons, don't spoil your life by living like cats and dogs and hogs. Utilize your valuable human life by accepting *tapasya*."

The question may then be, "Why this injunction? Why should I not live like an animal? Why do I have to live under the regulative principles of scriptures and saintly persons and the spiritual master?" Ṛṣabhadeva answers, *tapo divyaṁ putrakā yena sattvaṁ śuddhyet:* "My dear sons, if you accept this principle of *tapasya,* your existence will be purified." At present we are contaminated by the modes of material nature, mostly ignorance and passion. So Ṛṣabhadeva is advising his sons that if they abide by the instructions of scripture and so on, they will be purified of the lower modes of nature.

Then the question may be, "What is the use of purifying one's existence?" Ṛṣabhadeva answers, *yasmād brahma-saukhyaṁ tv anantam.* "When your existence is purified, you will be situated on the transcendental platform of blissful life, which is eternal." You are hankering after happiness. Why are you struggling so hard in this material existence? For happiness. Why are you after sense gratification? For happiness. Why do you want to possess so many things? For happiness. Why do you want to become beautiful. For happiness. Why do you want to eat so many things? For happiness. In every endeavor, happiness is your ultimate goal. But the happiness you are now deriving from material sources is temporary. You may become happy by intoxication, but for how long? That happiness is temporary. You may become happy by sex indulgence, but for how long? That happiness lasts for a few minutes or a few seconds. So if you want eternal, continuous happiness you have to purify your existential condition and place your self in the transcendental position; then you will enjoy eternal happiness.

This happiness is described in the *Padma Purāṇa* as follows:

ramante yogino 'nante
satyānande cid-ātmani
iti rāma-padenāsau
paraṁ brahmābhidhīyate

"The Supreme Absolute Truth is called Rāma because the transcendentalists enjoy [*ramante*] the unlimited true happiness of spiritual existence." So the transcendentalists are also enjoying sense gratification. But how? By serving the sense gratification of the Supreme, Param

Brahma. *Ramante* means "to enjoy sense gratification." For example, one of Kṛṣṇa's names is Rādhā-ramaṇa, "He who enjoys sense gratification with His eternal consort, Rādhārāṇī." So sense gratification is there in the transcendental position, but not this material sense gratification. Material sense gratification is a perverted reflection of spiritual sense gratification.

Devotional service is spiritual sense gratification: *hṛṣīkeṇa hṛṣīkeśa-sevanam. Hṛṣīka* means "senses." The master of the senses is Kṛṣṇa. So when you use your senses for Kṛṣṇa's sense gratification, you are in the transcendental position. And when you use your senses for your own sense gratification, that is material. This is the difference. So when you are situated on the transcendental platform, when your existence is purified by *tapasya* – by voluntarily accepting austerity and penance under the guidance of the spiritual master, the scriptures, and the saintly persons – at that time you will become fully satisfied by satisfying the senses of Kṛṣṇa.

The process is something like how the various parts of the body are nourished when we eat food. The different parts of the body depend on the stomach to enjoy food; they cannot enjoy food independently. Suppose you pick up a nice piece of cake with your fingers – the fingers cannot enjoy it independently. But if the fingers put it into the mouth and it goes to the stomach, then the stomach digests it and it turns into blood, and the heart circulates the blood to the different parts of the body, and your fingers are nourished. This is the process by which the fingers can enjoy the cake. Similarly, in devotional service sense gratification is there – but through serving Kṛṣṇa. Then you will feel complete satisfaction.

So real human life means to purify our present existential condition by voluntarily accepting the regulative principles given by the spiritual master, the scriptures, and the saintly persons. And when we become purified by employing our senses in the service of the Supreme Lord, we actually enjoy our senses.

Chapter Two

Serve the Great Souls

mahat-sevāṁ dvāram āhur vimuktes
tamo-dvāraṁ yoṣitāṁ saṅgi-saṅgam
mahāntas te sama-cittāḥ praśāntā
vimanyavaḥ suhṛdaḥ sādhavo ye

"One can attain the path of liberation from material bondage only by rendering service to highly advanced spiritual personalities. These personalities are impersonalists and devotees. Whether one wants to merge into the Lord's existence or wants to associate with the Personality of Godhead, one should render service to the *mahātmās*. For those who are not interested in such activities, who associate with people fond of women and sex, the path to hell is wide open. The *mahātmās* are equipoised. They do not see any difference between one living entity and another. They are very peaceful and are fully engaged in devotional service. They are devoid of anger, and they work for the benefit of everyone. They do not behave in any abominable way. Such people are known as *mahātmās.*"

Śrīmad-Bhāgavatam 5.5.2

The human body is like a junction. One may either take the path of liberation or the path leading to a hellish condition. How one can take these paths is described herein. On the path of liberation, one associates with *mahātmās,* and on the path of bondage one associates with those attached to sense gratification and women. There are two types of *mahātmās* – the impersonalist and the devotee. Although their ultimate goal is different, the process of emancipation is almost the same. Both want eternal happiness. One seeks happiness in impersonal Brahman, and the other seeks happiness in the association of the Supreme Personality of Godhead. As described in the first verse: *brahma-saukhyam.* Brahman means spiritual or eternal; both the impersonalist and the devotee seek eternal blissful life. In any case, it is advised that one become perfect. In the words of the *Caitanya-caritāmṛta* (*Madhya* 22.87):

asat-saṅga-tyāga, – ei vaiṣṇava-ācāra
'strī-saṅgī' – eka asādhu, 'kṛṣṇābhakta' āra

To remain unattached to the modes of material nature, one should avoid associating with those who are *asat,* materialistic. There are two kinds of materialists. One is attached to women and sense gratification, and the other is simply a nondevotee. On the positive side is association with *mahātmās,* and on the negative side is the avoidance of nondevotees and woman-hunters.

Who is a *mahātmā,* a great soul? In the *Bhagavad-gītā* (9.13) Kṛṣṇa says, *mahātmānas tu māṁ pārtha daivīṁ prakṛtim āśritāḥ*. A great soul is one who has taken shelter of God's spiritual nature, or spiritual energy, and from the presence of these energies we can understand that God exists, just as we can understand from the presence of the sunlight that the sun has risen in the sky. Light is simply the energy of the sun, so in the morning, as soon as you look through your window and see that there is light in the sky, you can understand that the sun has risen. Similarly, we can understand the existence of God by the presence of His spiritual and material energies. Otherwise, where have these energies come from? As stated in the *Viṣṇu Purāṇa:*

eka-deśa sthitasyāgner
jyotsnā vistāriṇī yathā
parasya brahmaṇaḥ śaktis
tathedam akhilaṁ jagat

"Just as a fire situated in one place spreads its illumination all over, so the Supreme Personality of Godhead, Parabrahman, spreads His energies all over the universe." So, in this verse, spoken by Ṛṣabhadeva, the words *mahat* and *mahāntas* refer to the *mahātmās,* those who have taken shelter of the Lord's spiritual energy. If one wants to be liberated from the entanglement of material life – from the miseries of birth, death, old age, disease, and so many other sufferings – one has to serve such a great saintly person and execute austerities under his direction.

And how can you understand who has taken shelter of the Lord's spiritual energy? Ṛṣabhadeva says *mahāntas te sama-cittāḥ:* "The *mahātmās* are always equipoised, seeing everyone equally." As Lord Kṛṣṇa says in the *Bhagavad-gītā* (5.18):

vidyā-vinaya-sampanne
brāhmaṇe gavi hastini
śuni caiva śva-pāke ca
paṇḍitāḥ sama-darśinaḥ

"The humble sage, by virtue of true knowledge, sees with equal vision a learned and gentle *brāhmaṇa,* a cow, an elephant, a dog, and a dog-eater [outcaste]." The *mahātmā* is equally disposed to everyone. He doesn't think, "He is American, so I shall be kind to him," or "He is Indian, so I shall be kind to him," or "He is black, so I shall be kind to him." No. He is kind to everyone.

Another quality of the *mahātmā* is that he is *praśānta,* always very peaceful. Because he knows himself to be pure spirit, an eternal servant of Kṛṣṇa, he cannot be disturbed by any material condition. Also, he is *vimanyava,* free of anger, and *suhṛdaḥ,* a well-wisher for everyone. That is the vision of the *mahātmā*. He sees that people are suffering without God consciousness, without understanding their relationship with God, and so he tries to teach them. Therefore he has to be tolerant (*titikṣava*). When he tries to teach people about Kṛṣṇa consciousness, there will be so many insults, so many inconveniences. He has to tolerate them without becoming disturbed. In the Western countries Lord Jesus Christ perfectly showed this quality of tolerance. Because he was preaching about God consciousness, the state ordered that he be crucified. Still, he prayed to God, "Please excuse them." So peacefulness, seeing everyone equally, freedom from anger, tolerance, mercy – these are the characteristics of a *mahātmā* or *sādhu,* a saintly person.

So we have to find such a person, associate with him, and serve him in full surrender. As Lord Kṛṣṇa says in the *Bhagavad-gītā* (4.34):

tad viddhi praṇipātena
paripraśnena sevayā
upadekṣyanti te jñānaṁ
jñāninas tattva-darśinaḥ

"Just try to learn the truth by approaching a spiritual master. Inquire from him submissively and render service unto him. The self-realized soul can impart knowledge unto you because he has seen the truth."

On the opposite side from service to the *sādhus* is *yoṣitāṁ saṅgi-saṅgam,* association with those who are too much attached to women. Actually, *yoṣitām* refers to anything enjoyable. There are so many things that attract us. Each sense has its own object of enjoyment. The eyes want to see beautiful forms. The tongue wants to enjoy very tasty food. The ears are attracted to nice singing. The nostrils are attracted to sweet fragrances. And the skin wants to touch soft things. All these are *yoṣitām,* enjoyable things, and people in general are attracted to all of them. They are going to the cinema, drinking wine, going to restaurants and clubs, and so on. And if we associate with persons who are attached to all these things for sense gratification, then the door to hell opens for us.

So you have to choose which door you will enter: one door leads to liberation from the entanglement of repeated birth and death and places us on the path back home, back to Godhead, and the other door, the door of sense gratification, leads to darkness (*adānta-gobhir viśatāṁ tamisram*). The more we indulge in sense gratification or associate with those who indulge in sense gratification, the deeper we go down into hellish life.

Chapter Three

Achieving Unending Happiness

ye vā mayīśe kṛta-sauhṛdārthā
janeṣu dehambhara-vārtikeṣu
gṛheṣu jāyātmaja-rātimatsu
na prīti-yuktā yāvad-arthāś ca loke

"Those who are interested in reviving Kṛṣṇa consciousness and increasing their love of Godhead do not like to do anything that is not related to Kṛṣṇa. They are not interested in mingling with people who are busy maintaining their bodies, eating, sleeping, mating, and defending. They are not attached to their homes, although they may be householders. Nor are they attached to wives, children, friends, or wealth. At the same time, they are not indifferent to the execution of their duties. Such people are interested in collecting only enough money to keep the body and soul together."

Śrīmad-Bhāgavatam 5.5.3

Whether he is an impersonalist or a devotee, one who is actually interested in advancing spiritually should not mingle with those who are simply interested in maintaining the body by means of the so-called advancement of civilization. Those who are interested in spiritual life should not be attached to homely comforts in the company of wife, children, friends, and so forth. Even if one is a *gṛhastha* and has to earn his livelihood, he should be satisfied by collecting only enough money to maintain body and soul together. One should not have more than that nor less than that. As indicated herein, a householder should endeavor to earn money for the execution of *bhakti-yoga* – *śravaṇaṁ kīrtanaṁ viṣṇoḥ smaraṇaṁ pāda-sevanam / arcanaṁ vandanaṁ dāsyaṁ sakhyam ātma-nivedanam.* A householder should lead such a life that he gets full opportunity to hear and chant. He should worship the Deity at home, observe festivals, and invite friends in and give them *prasāda*. A householder should earn money for this purpose, not for sense gratification.

Generally, however, people are interested only in maintaining their bodies. *Śrīmad-Bhāgavatam* (2.1.3) says:

nidrayā hriyate naktaṁ
vyavāyena ca vā vayaḥ
divā cārthehayā rājan
kuṭumba-bharaṇena vā

At night they waste time by sleeping or indulging in sex, and during the daytime they are very busy trying to get some money. And as soon as they get money, they spend it to maintain their families. So where it the time for Kṛṣṇa consciousness? There is no time.

One should not be interested in mixing with those who are busy only with bodily affairs. One may be a householder, but one should be interested in devotional service to Kṛṣṇa, not simply in maintaining one's family. Such a householder *mahātmā* has no desire to associate with those who are interested only in bodily affairs. His only desire is to cultivate friendship with Kṛṣṇa (*ye vā mayīśe kṛta-sauhṛdārthā*). Then what about his family? Yes, he has his home, his wife, his children, and means for earning money – but he's not very much interested. Officially he fulfills his family obligations, but his primary interest is Kṛṣṇa consciousness.

Of course, the householder *mahātmā* does not neglect his family responsibilities. He takes care of his children, his wife – everything – but with a spirit of detachment: *anāsaktasya viṣayān yathārham upayuñjataḥ*. It is required that you educate your children and maintain your wife, but at the same time you should cultivate detachment. One should not think, "I shall sacrifice everything for my wife, children, and home." That is not a *mahātmā's* idea, because he knows that he cannot improve their destiny. Everyone has received a body with a destiny that he cannot change. So the scripture says, *tasyaiva hetoḥ prayateta kovido na labhyate yad bhramatām upary adhaḥ:* The wise person should try for advancement in Kṛṣṇa consciousness, not for material advancement. You may think, "If I work very hard, I shall improve my material position," but that is not possible. Your material position is already fixed. No one strives for distress, but distress comes automatically according to destiny. Similarly, if you have happiness in your destiny, it will come automatically, as the distress comes (*tal labhyate duḥkhavad anyataḥ sukham*). So don't be misled by material happiness and distress. They are already fixed. Simply try to advance in Kṛṣṇa consciousness and achieve unending transcendental happiness (*brahma-saukhyam tv anantam*). That is your real business.

Chapter Four

The Pain of Fleshly Pleasures

nūnaṁ pramattaḥ kurute vikarma
yad indriya-prītaya āpṛṇoti
na sādhu manye yata ātmano 'yam
asann api kleśada āsa dehaḥ

"When a person considers sense gratification the aim of life, he certainly becomes mad after materialistic living and engages in all kinds of sinful activity. He does not know that due to his past misdeeds he has already received a body which, although temporary, is the cause of his misery. Actually the living entity should not have taken on a material body, but he has been awarded the material body for sense gratification. Therefore I think it not befitting an intelligent man to involve himself again in the activities of sense gratification by which he perpetually gets material bodies one after another."

Śrīmad-Bhāgavatam 5.5.4

Begging, borrowing, and stealing to live for sense gratification is condemned in this verse because such consciousness leads one to a dark, hellish condition. The four sinful activities are illicit sex, meat-eating, intoxication, and gambling. These are the means by which one gets another material body that is full of miseries. In the *Vedas* it is said: *asaṅgo hy ayaṁ puruṣaḥ*. The living entity is not really connected with this material world, but due to his tendency to enjoy the material senses he is put into the material condition. One should perfect his life by associating with devotees. He should not become further implicated in the material body.

Here materialistic persons are described as *pramattaḥ,* "extremely mad or intoxicated." They're running here and there in their motorcars. From five o'clock in the morning or even earlier, the main roads are full of motorcars. And what is the aim of such materialistic persons? *Yad indriya-prītaya āpṛṇoti:* their aim is to satisfy their senses. Eat, drink, be merry, and enjoy – that's all. Get money, go to the restaurant, go to the liquor shop, go to the prostitute house and the nightclub. They do not know anything more than *indriya-prīti,* sense gratification.

So they are all mad, and they are being implicated in so many sinful activities due to their desires for sense gratification. The result is that they get another material body after death. Everyone gets a certain type of body according to his sins and his specific desires for sense gratification. Otherwise, why are there so many varieties of life? Why is one soul born as a human being, another as a pig, another as a demigod, another as a tree, another as a fish? These varieties of life are all due to different desires for sense gratification and degrees of implication in sinful activities. Kṛṣṇa resides within the heart as the Supersoul, and he knows our desires and activities. As He says in the *Bhagavad-gītā* (18.61):

īśvaraḥ sarva-bhūtānāṁ
hṛd-deśe 'rjuna tiṣṭhati
bhrāmayan sarva-bhūtāni
yantrārūḍhāni māyayā

"The *īśvara,* the Supreme Lord, is situated in everyone's heart as the Supersoul, O Arjuna, and is directing the wanderings of all living entities, who are seated as on a machine, made of the material energy." The materialist is always thinking, "If I would have acted like this, I would have gotten that opportunity, and then I would have enjoyed like this ..." This kind of thinking is going on continually. And it is God's business – His thankless business – to note down, "All right, the rascal wants to enjoy like this, so I will give him such a facility." He's so merciful that He orders *māyā,* the material nature, "Give him such-and-such body so he can enjoy as he wants." Therefore we see so many varieties of bodies. They are all due to varieties of desire.

Unfortunately, all of these bodies are sources of misery (*kleśada*). Anyone who has a material body must suffer. Even the millionaire must suffer. There was once a very rich man in Kolkata who could hardly eat. He had no appetite. He was served sumptuous food simply as a show but he could not eat it. One day he saw a poor man passing on the street, carrying a fish and singing jubilantly. The rich gentleman said, "I am a rich man, but I have no appetite for all the many opulent foods that are served to me. Yet that poor man is thinking how he'll go home and cook his fish and eat it very nicely. He is so jubilant! If I would have been that poor man, at least I could have enjoyed some food." In spite of his becoming rich he could not gratify his senses. His body was simply a source of misery.

So if you want to stop these varieties of material bodies, then you should give up all your nonsensical material desires. We already have a body that is a source of misery. Everyone has experience. No one can say, "My body never feels pain. I am perfect." That is not possible. As soon as you get a material body, it must be subjected to so many sufferings. Tribulations there must be. Therefore you should try to stop getting these material bodies. And to do this you must practice devotional service to Kṛṣṇa. Otherwise, you will continue on the path of birth and death. As Kṛṣṇa states in the *Bhagavad-gītā* (9.3):

aśraddadhānāḥ puruṣā
dharmasyāsya paran-tapa
aprāpya māṁ nivartante
mṛtyu-saṁsāra-vartmani

If you have no faith in the process of Kṛṣṇa consciousness you cannot attain Kṛṣṇa, and then you must continue on the path of birth and death – getting one body and again dying, getting another body and again dying.

In the modern age, education in these subjects is practically nil. It is very regrettable. But the information is there in the Vedic scriptures. And one who is intelligent will take advantage of this science, Kṛṣṇa consciousness, and mold his life accordingly so that he can stop this process of repeatedly accepting a body that is *kleśada,* the source of all miseries. That is the perfection of life.

Chapter Five

Inquire Into the Absolute

parābhavas tāvad abodha-jāto
yāvan na jijñāsata ātma-tattvam
yāvat kriyās tāvad idaṁ mano vai
karmātmakaṁ yena śarīra-bandhaḥ

"As long as one does not inquire about the spiritual values of life, one is defeated and subjected to miseries arising from ignorance. Be it sinful or pious, karma has its resultant actions. If a person is engaged in any kind of karma, his mind is called *karmātmaka,* colored with fruitive activity. As long as the mind is impure, consciousness is unclear, and as long as one is absorbed in fruitive activity, he has to accept a material body."

Śrīmad-Bhāgavatam 5.5.5

Generally people think that one should act very piously in order to be relieved from misery, but this is not a fact. Even though one engages in pious activity and speculation, he is nonetheless defeated. His only aim should be emancipation from the clutches of *māyā* and all material activities. Speculative knowledge and pious activity do not solve the problems of material life. One should be inquisitive to understand his spiritual position. As stated in *Bhagavad-gītā* (4.37):

yathaidhāṁsi samiddho 'gnir
bhasma-sāt kurute 'rjuna
jñānāgniḥ sarva-karmāṇi
bhasma-sāt kurute tathā

"As a blazing fire turns firewood to ashes, O Arjuna, so does the fire of knowledge burn to ashes all reactions to material activities."

Unless one understands the self and its activities, one has to be considered in material bondage. In *Śrīmad-Bhāgavatam* (10.2.32) it is also said: *ye 'nye 'ravindākṣa vimukta-māninas tvayy asta-bhāvād aviśuddha-buddhayaḥ.* A person who doesn't have knowledge of devotional service may think himself liberated, but actually he is not. *Āruhya kṛcchreṇa paraṁ padaṁ tataḥ patanty adho 'nādṛta-yuṣmad-aṅghrayaḥ:* such people may approach the impersonal Brahman effulgence, but they fall down again into material enjoyment because they have no knowledge of devotional service. As long as one is interested in karma and *jñāna,* he continues enduring the miseries of material life – birth, old age, disease, and death. *Karmīs* certainly take on one body after another. As far as *jñānīs* are concerned, unless they are promoted to the topmost understanding, they must return to the material world. As explained in the *Bhagavad-gītā* (7.19): *bahūnāṁ janma-nām ante jñānavān māṁ prapadyate.* The point is to know Kṛṣṇa, Vāsudeva, as everything and surrender unto Him. *Karmīs* do not know this, but a devotee who is one hundred percent engaged in the devotional service of the Lord knows fully what is karma and *jñāna;* therefore a pure devotee is no longer interested in karma or *jñāna. Anyābhilāṣitā-śūnyaṁ jñāna-karmādy-anāvṛtam.* The real *bhakta* is untouched by any tinge of karma and *jñāna.* His only purpose in life is to serve the Lord. Therefore his mind is always engaged in thoughts of Kṛṣṇa, and he is free from bondage to a material body (*śarīra-bandhaḥ*). The material body is actually a great impediment to the soul, but in the modern so-called civilization there is no education on these matters.

In the state of bondage, whatever you do for your so-called material progress is ultimately defeated (*parābhava*). People are busily engaged throughout the day and night, thinking they are making material progress. But it is not progress; it is regression. This they do not know. Why? Because they never inquire into *ātma-tattva,* the spiritual values of life. Even big, big professors think that they have received their body by accident and that as soon as the body is finished, everything is finished. That means they do not know the first lesson of *ātma-tattva* – that the soul, or self, is eternal. And on the basis of this misconception they are inventing so many "isms" – communism, altruism, humanitarianism, etc.

Recently we talked with a medical man who was working on a cure for leprosy. That is good, but why should there be leprosy in the first place? Why is one man suffering from leprosy and another not suffering? Who is making this arrangement? These questions modern people do not ask, because they have become dull. And therefore whatever plans they make are baffled after some time (*parābhava*). They do not know what plans they should make for their ultimate benefit. For example, a child will think, "If I play like this, it will be very nice." So he engages in one type of play. And then he becomes dissatisfied and gives up that play and engages in another type of play. Out of ignorance (*abodha*), the child does not know where to find lasting happiness.

To dissipate this ignorance, one has to approach a person who is not *abodha* but *bodha,* full of knowledge. Such a person is called a *budhā,* a wise man, because he knows the real goal of life and how to attain it. This word *budhā* is where Lord Buddha's name comes from. He understood everything. At first he was not a *budhā* – he was a prince, and he never came out of the palace. But one day he left the palace and saw an old man with a walking stick walking with great difficulty. So he inquired from his servants: "What is this?" "This is an old man," they replied, "Everyone has to become like this." That was the inspiration for him to seek understanding. He inquired, "Why should he be like that? Why should one have to become an old man and be forced to walk with a stick?" So these inquiries made him a *budhā,* and he became Lord Buddha through meditation. Of course, that was his pastime. But he showed by example how inquisitiveness into the ultimate causes of suffering can lead one to proper knowledge. And where to get that proper knowledge? From a guru. The *Vedas* say, *tad-vijñānārthaṁ sa gurum evābhigacchet:* "If you want proper knowledge of the Absolute Truth, you must approach a bona fide guru."

People should be encouraged to inquire from the guru about the process for realizing the Absolute Truth: *sad-dharma pṛcchāt*. The student should be eager to know. It is not that one should accept the guru as a fashion. Nowadays many people do that. "Everyone has a dog, and everyone has a guru. So let me keep a guru." That is not the way to real understanding. One should be very inquisitive, but one should also serve the guru. As Kṛṣṇa says in the *Bhagavad-gītā* (4.34):

tad viddhi praṇipātena
paripraśnena sevayā
upadekṣyanti te jñānaṁ
jñāninas tattva-darśinaḥ

"Just try to learn the truth by approaching a spiritual master. Inquire from him submissively and render service unto him. The self-realized soul can impart knowledge unto you because he has seen the truth." You must be ready to serve the guru. Then you have the right to ask questions. First you must find a person to whom you can fully surrender (*praṇipātena*). Then you can inquire from him about *ātma-tattva,* spiritual science. And the inquiry should be accompanied by service. The more service you render to the guru, the more the truth is revealed.

yasya deve parā bhaktir
yathā deve tathā gurau

tasyaite kathitā hy arthāḥ
prakāśante mahātmanaḥ

"Only unto those great souls who have unflinching devotion to the Lord and to the spiritual master is transcendental knowledge revealed."

Chapter Six

Freedom Through Divine Love

evaṁ manaḥ karma-vaśaṁ prayuṅkte
avidyayātmany upadhīyamāne
prītir na yāvan mayi vāsudeve
na mucyate deha-yogena tāvat

"When the living entity is covered by the mode of ignorance, he does not understand the individual living being and the supreme living being, and his mind is subjugated by fruitive activity. Therefore, until one has love for Lord Vāsudeva, who is none other than Myself, he is certainly not delivered from having to accept a material body again and again."

Śrīmad-Bhāgavatam 5.5.6

When the mind is polluted by fruitive activity, the living entity wants to be elevated from one material position to another. Generally everyone is involved in working hard day and night to improve his economic condition. Even when one understands the Vedic rituals, he becomes interested in promotion to heavenly planets, not knowing that one's real interest lies in returning home, back to Godhead. By acting on the platform of fruitive activity, one wanders throughout the universe in different species and forms. Unless he comes in contact with a devotee of the Lord, a guru, he does not become attached to the service of Lord Vāsudeva. Knowledge of Vāsudeva requires many births to understand. As confirmed in *Bhagavad-gītā* (7.19): *vāsudevaḥ sarvam iti sa mahātmā sudurlabhaḥ*. After struggling for existence for many births one may take shelter at the lotus feet of Vāsudeva, Kṛṣṇa. When this happens, one actually becomes wise and surrenders unto Him. That is the only way to stop the repetition of birth and death. This is confirmed in *Śrī Caitanya-caritāmṛta* (*Madhya* 19.151) in the instructions given by Śrī Caitanya Mahāprabhu to Śrīla Rūpa Gosvāmī at Daśāśvamedha-ghāṭa.

brahmāṇḍa bhramite kona bhāgyavān jīva
guru-kṛṣṇa-prasāde pāya bhakti-latā-bīja

The living entity wanders throughout different planets in different forms and bodies, but if by chance he comes in contact with a bona fide spiritual master, by the grace of the spiritual master he receives Lord Kṛṣṇa's shelter, and his devotional life begins.

In material life the living entity's problem is contact with the material body. But nobody knows this.

Especially these days people cannot understand that the material body is foreign to us and that we are entrapped within it and victimized by it. This is our real problem. But because of *avidyā,* ignorance, people do not know this. *Avidyā* is very strong when one is in the mode of passion (*rajo-guṇa*) or ignorance (*tamo-guṇa*). In the mode of goodness (*sattva-guṇa*) there is illumination. This means one has acquired brahminical qualifications. In that state one can understand, "I am not this body; I am different from it." For those in the mode of goodness, it is easier to advance in devotional life.

Human civilization should not drag someone in the mode of goodness down to the mode of ignorance. But the modern civilization does that. The allurements of the modern material civilization are so strong and so bad that even those who by previous pious activities are born in good families are being dragged down to sinful behavior. They are learning how to drink, how to eat meat, how to have illicit sex. These are the symptoms of the lowest type of ignorance. Real civilization means elevation. In other words, human civilization should be so arranged that everyone is gradually drawn to the mode of goodness, not dragged down to the mode of ignorance. But today the social, political, and economic arrangements are so bad that everyone is being dragged down to the mode of ignorance. This is not civilization. It is degradation. The aim of human life is to become liberated from the material body, and a civilization that elevates people to that platform is a real human civilization. Otherwise it is not civilization but animal life.

The Kṛṣṇa consciousness movement is attempting to

bring human society to the platform of actual civilization. It is a very scientific movement. Here Lord Ṛṣabhadeva says, *prītir na yāvan mayi vāsudeve na mucyate deha-yogena tāvat:* "Until one develops love for Me, Vāsudeva, one will not be liberated from the material body." Since our problem is entrapment in the material body, we need a process by which we can develop love for Vāsudeva, or Kṛṣṇa, so we can be liberated from the body. That process is *bhakti,* or devotional service. One who follows the process of devotional service gradually comes to the platform of loving Kṛṣṇa. That is civilization – to bring one to the platform of loving Kṛṣṇa.

Real love means that one sees the beloved as everything (*vāsudevaṁ sarvam iti*). In this material world the closest thing we find to real love is a mother's love for her child. The mother loves the child so intensely that she is always anxious to take care of the child and her whole attention is on the child. From such an example we can understand something about real love, love for Kṛṣṇa. Material so-called love does not last, but nature dictates that you love your child, you love your husband, you love your wife, your country, your society. There are different varieties of love. But when that love is concentrated on Vāsudeva, Kṛṣṇa, it is the highest perfection of life.

You have to come to the stage of being firmly convinced that "Kṛṣṇa is my life." The highest perfection of this consciousness is displayed in Vṛndāvana, especially by the *gopīs*. Everyone in Vṛndāvana is attached to Kṛṣṇa – even the trees and plants, even the grains of sand. One cannot all of a sudden attain that highest stage of consciousness, but if one practices *bhakti-yoga* as we are teaching it, that stage will develop gradually. The proof is the success of this Kṛṣṇa consciousness movement. All over the world people who had never heard of Kṛṣṇa, who were in the lowest states of ignorance, are taking to Kṛṣṇa consciousness, and their love for Kṛṣṇa is gradually increasing. That is natural. As it is said in the *Caitanya-caritāmṛta* (*Madhya* 22.107):

nitya-siddha kṛṣṇa-prema 'sādhya' kabhu naya
śravaṇādi-śuddha-citte karaye udaya

"Pure love for Kṛṣṇa is eternally established in the hearts of the living entities. It is not something to be gained from another source. When the heart is purified by hearing and chanting about Kṛṣṇa, this love naturally awakens." Just as we are all eternal as living entities, so our devotion to Kṛṣṇa is eternal. Now it is simply covered by *avidyā,* ignorance. When we forget Kṛṣṇa, that is *avidyā,* and as soon as we take Kṛṣṇa as our life and soul, that is *vidyā. Avidyā* is darkness; *vidyā* is light. The Vedic injunction is *tamasi mā jyotir gama:* "Don't keep yourself in the darkness of ignorance; come to the light [*jyoti*] of Kṛṣṇa consciousness."

Ultimately that *jyoti* means love for Kṛṣṇa and the loving affairs of Kṛṣṇa in the spiritual world. That world is *jyotirmaya-dhāma,* Kṛṣṇa's self-effulgent abode. Just as in the sun there is no question of darkness, in the spiritual world there is also no question of darkness or ignorance. Everyone and everything there is in the state of *śuddha-sattva,* pure goodness. Not only goodness, but *pure* goodness. Here in this material world there are three modes – goodness, passion, and ignorance. None of these modes is pure; each is mixed with the others. And because there is a mixture, we see so many varieties of living beings. But we have to come to the platform of *śuddha-sattva,* pure goodness. The best process for this is hearing about Kṛṣṇa from authorized sources. The *Śrīmad-Bhāgavatam* (1.2.17) explains:

śṛṇvatāṁ sva-kathāḥ kṛṣṇaḥ
puṇya-śravaṇa-kīrtanaḥ
hṛdy antaḥ stho hy abhadrāṇi
vidhunoti suhṛt satām

"Śrī Kṛṣṇa, the Supreme Personality of Godhead, who is the Supersoul in everyone's heart and the benefactor of the truthful devotee, cleanses desire for material enjoyment from the heart of the devotee who has developed the urge to hear His messages, which are in themselves virtuous when properly heard and chanted." So if you seriously hear and chant about Kṛṣṇa, thinking, "In this life I shall strive with great determination only to increase my love for Kṛṣṇa," it can be done. And as soon as you fully develop your love for Kṛṣṇa, there is no longer a chance of your being entrapped in a material body.

Chapter Seven

Don't Waste Time on Sense Pleasure

yadā na paśyaty ayathā guṇehāṁ
svārthe pramattaḥ sahasā vipaścit
gata-smṛtir vindati tatra tāpān
āsādya maithunyam agāram ajñaḥ

"Even though one may be very learned and wise, he is mad if he does not understand that the endeavor for sense gratification is a useless waste of time. Being forgetful of his own interest, he tries to be happy in the material world, centering his interests around his home, which is based on sexual intercourse and which brings him all kinds of material miseries. In this way one is no better than a foolish animal."

Śrīmad-Bhāgavatam 5.5.7

In the lowest stage of devotional life, one is not an unalloyed devotee. *Anyābhilāṣitā-śūnyaṁ jñāna-karmādy-anāvṛtam:* to be an unalloyed devotee, one must be freed from all material desires and untouched by fruitive activity and speculative knowledge. On the lower platform, one may sometimes be interested in philosophical speculation with a tinge of devotion. However, at that stage one is still interested in sense gratification and is contaminated by the modes of material nature. The influence of *māyā* is so strong that even a person advanced in knowledge actually forgets that he is Kṛṣṇa's eternal servant. Therefore he remains satisfied in his householder life, which is centered around sexual intercourse. Conceding to a life of sex, he agrees to suffer all kinds of material miseries. Due to ignorance, one is thus bound by the chain of material laws.

Our real self-interest (*svārtha*) is to break these chains, but to understand this one has to be *vipaścit,* learned. Whether one is a fruitive worker, a speculator, a yogi, or a devotee, everyone is working for what he considers his self-interest. But for the devotees there is a little difference; they work for Superself-interest while others work for individual self-interest. The difference between working for self-interest and working for Superself-interest is the difference between lust and love, or *prema.* In the *Caitanya-caritāmṛta* (*Ādi* 4.165), Kṛṣṇadāsa Kavirāja Gosvāmī has clearly explained this difference:

ātmendriya-prīti-vāñchā – tāre bali 'kāma'
kṛṣṇendriya-prīti-icchā dhare 'prema' nāma

"When one desires his personal sense gratification, that is *kāma,* or lust, and when one wants to satisfy the senses of Kṛṣṇa, that is *prema,* or love." The contrast between lust and love is shown in the *Bhagavad-gītā*. At the beginning of the *Bhagavad-gītā* Arjuna was thinking, "How can I possibly kill my brother, my nephews, my master, my teacher, my grandfather? I cannot do it; I refuse to fight." This calculation – in terms of the interest of his family and teacher – was for Arjuna's personal sense gratification. In other words, it was for his self-interest. But at the end of the *Bhagavad-gītā,* when Arjuna agreed to satisfy Kṛṣṇa by fighting, he was acting for Superself-interest. Arjuna had gone from *kāma* to *prema*.

For the materialistic person there are two kinds of self-interest. One is concentrated and the other is extended. If you give a child a piece of cake, his immediate impulse is to eat it all himself, but if he is a little liberal he will give some to his friend. While the child is eating, his friend says, "Oh, you are eating cake? Give me some." "All right," the child replies, "you can take some." At first the child shows concentrated self-interest and then extended self-interest. Another example is the big political leader. He is primarily interested in the welfare of himself and his family members – after all, self-preservation is the first law of nature – but he also works for the benefit of all members of the community, society, or country. But such extended self-interest can never be perfect, because there is always some fight between one community and another community, one society and another society, and one nation and another nation. Only when that extended self-interest reaches up to Viṣṇu is it perfect. Then it is genuine self-interest, or Superself-interest.

Unfortunately, today people have no idea that serving the Supreme Lord, Viṣṇu or Kṛṣṇa, is their ultimate self-interest (*na te viduḥ svārtha-gatiṁ hi viṣṇum*). They think that if one extends his self-interest to his country, or even to all humanity, he will become a big man and people will honor him for his philanthropy. But that is not real philanthropy. Real philanthropy is serving Kṛṣṇa's interest. Otherwise it is all *kāma,* lust. Today's so-called philanthropy, altruism, and humanitarianism are all imperfect because they do not serve our ultimate self-interest. Again we can use the example of the cake. Suppose we pick up a nice piece of cake with our fingers. If the fingers think, "Now we have got it; we shall enjoy it ourselves," the cake will be spoiled. But if the fingers place it in the mouth, then their own interest will actually be served. As soon as the cake goes to the stomach, the energy is distributed not only to the fingers of the right hand but to those of the left hand also, and in fact to the whole body. Similarly, when one serves Kṛṣṇa's interest, everyone's interest is served because Kṛṣṇa is the root of everything. This law people do not know. Therefore here Lord Ṛṣabhadeva says, *svārthe pramattaḥ:* people do not know their real self-interest. Although everyone is trying individually, communally, and nationally to serve their self-interest, they do not know that their real self-interest lies in serving Kṛṣṇa.

Only in the human form of life can we understand our real self-interest. As Prahlāda Mahārāja says (7.6.1):

kaumāra ācaret prājño
dharmān bhāgavatān iha

durlabhaṁ mānuṣaṁ janma
tad apy adhruvam arthadam

"One who is sufficiently intelligent should use the human form of body from the very beginning of life – in other words, from the tender age of childhood – to practice the activities of devotional service, giving up all other engagements. The human body is most rarely achieved, and although temporary like other bodies, it is meaningful because in human life one can perform devotional service. Even a slight amount of sincere devotional service can give one complete perfection." As for physiological, anatomical, and even psychological construction, the human body is little different from the dog's. The dog has senses and we have senses; the dog has a mind and we have a mind; the dog has intelligence and we also have intelligence; the dog eats and we also eat; the dog sleeps and we also sleep. Similarly, if you cut an animal's body there will be blood, and if you cut a man's body there will also be blood. But the difference is that an animal cannot understand his real self-interest while a human being can. And if you act accordingly you can make your life successful. That is the special advantage of the human form of life. We should not waste it. As Narottama Dāsa Ṭhākura has sung, taking the role of a conditioned soul:

hari hari! viphale janama goṅāinu
manuṣya-janama pāiyā, rādhā-kṛṣṇa nā bhajiyā,
jāniyā śuniyā viṣa khāinu

"O Lord Kṛṣṇa, I have wasted my life. Although I have taken this rare human birth, I have not served Rādhā and Kṛṣṇa, and thus I have knowingly drunk poison." Sometimes we may take poison unknowingly – food poison or some other poison – but if one takes poison *knowingly,* that means he's killing himself. Similarly, in this human form of life, if we do not come to the understanding that without Kṛṣṇa consciousness our life is wasted we are simply taking poison. Then our life is spoiled. We will be put into a miserable condition birth after birth. That is nature's way. You cannot escape the stringent laws of material nature. As Kṛṣṇa states in the *Bhagavad-gītā* (9.3):

aśraddadhānāḥ puruṣā
dharmasyāsya paran-tapa
aprāpya māṁ nivartante
mṛtyu-saṁsāra-vartmani

"Those who are not faithful in this devotional service cannot attain Me, O conqueror of enemies. Therefore they return to the path of birth and death in this material world." On account of false prestige, false knowledge, and false education, people think they are independent of God, that they can do whatever they like. We have to give up this mentality; otherwise we will have to continue in the miserable cycle of birth and death because we have forgotten our real position.

Here Lord Ṛṣabhadeva states that the main reason people foolishly forget their position as servants of Kṛṣṇa and suffer material pangs is sex: *maithunyam agāram ajñaḥ*. We see people working so hard day and night. Sometimes they start for their business or office as early as five in the morning and do not return until ten o'clock at night. Why are they working so hard? For the pleasure of sex indulgence, that's all. Their main happiness is enjoying sexual intercourse at night. Prahlāda Mahārāja states that the pleasures a materialistic householder enjoys, centered on sex, are very insignificant (*tuccham*). Indeed, such a person's home becomes a prison house (*agāra*), and he remains shackled by the iron chains of sex. Only a fool would accept this lowest class of happiness as the aim of life. So don't be foolish; be intelligent and understand that your real self-interest lies in worshiping Kṛṣṇa.

Chapter Eight

Sex Is the Main Cause of Bondage

puṁsaḥ striyā mithunī-bhāvam etaṁ
tayor mitho hṛdaya-granthim āhuḥ
ato gṛha-kṣetra-sutāpta-vittair
janasya moho 'yam ahaṁ mameti

"The attraction between male and female is the basic principle of material existence. On the basis of this misconception, which ties together the hearts of the male and female, one becomes attracted to his body, home, property, children, relatives, and wealth. In this way one increases life's illusions and thinks in terms of 'I and mine.'"

Śrīmad-Bhāgavatam 5.5.8

Sex serves as the natural attraction between man and woman, and when they are married, their relationship becomes more involved. Due to the entangling relationship between man and woman, there is a sense of illusion whereby one thinks, "This man is my husband," or "This woman is my wife." This is called *hṛdaya-granthi,* "the hard knot in the heart." This knot is very difficult to undo, even though a man and woman separate either for the principles of *varṇāśrama* or simply to get a divorce. In any case, the man always thinks of the woman, and the woman always thinks of the man. Thus a person becomes materially attached to family, property, and children, although all of these are temporary. The possessor, unfortunately, identifies with his property and wealth. Sometimes, even after renunciation one becomes attached to a temple or to the few things that constitute the property of a *sannyāsī,* but such attachment is not as strong as family attachment. The attachment to the family is the strongest illusion. In the *Satya-saṁhitā* it is stated:

brahmādyā yājñavalkādyā
mucyante strī-sahāyinaḥ
bodhyante kecanaiteṣāṁ
viśeṣam ca vido viduḥ

Sometimes it is found among exalted personalities like Lord Brahmā that the wife and children are not a cause of bondage. On the contrary, the wife actually helps further spiritual life and liberation. Nonetheless, most people are bound by the knots of the marital relationship, and consequently they forget their relationship with Kṛṣṇa.

So sex attraction is the beginning of the illusion summarized in the phrase *ahaṁ mameti:* "I am my body, and everything in relationship to my body is mine." A man searches after a woman, and a woman searches after a man, and when they unite for sex the material illusion becomes very strong. This is nature's arrangement for keeping the conditioned soul under her stringent laws. As it is said:

kṛṣṇa-bahirmukha haiyā bhoga-vāñchā kare
nikaṭa-stha māyā tāre jāpaṭiyā dhare

"As soon as one becomes inimical to Kṛṣṇa and desires sense gratification, he is immediately struck down by the illusory energy of the Lord." This is just like breaking the laws of the state. We have practical experience that as soon as we refuse to obey the state laws we immediately become criminals and are subjected to prosecution and imprisonment. Just as you cannot defy the state laws without being punished by the government, you cannot defy Kṛṣṇa's laws without being punished by the laws of nature. But because we are in illusion, we think our effort to diminish this punishment is advancement of civilization.

The whole material world is based on the attraction between male and female. This principle is working not only in human society but among the birds, beasts, aquatics, insects – everywhere. You will find that as soon as a male pigeon sees a female pigeon, the male immediately begins canvassing, "Please come, and let us unite." This is nature's way. Therefore, in human society one has to understand by Vedic knowledge, by education, that we are bound up within this material world due to sex attraction. Both the male and the female want to be the enjoyer. Nobody is thinking "I shall be enjoyed." Everyone is thinking, "I shall enjoy." Nobody wants to be predominated; everyone wants to be the predominator. This is illusion.

The Kṛṣṇa consciousness movement is teaching everyone to give up this idea of being the predominator and learn how to be predominated by the Supreme Lord, Kṛṣṇa – just the opposite of the illusory materialistic idea. Kṛṣṇa comes personally and says, "Why are you trying to be the predominator? That is not possible. I am the predominator. Just surrender to Me and you will be happy." *Sarva-dharmān parityajya mām ekaṁ śaraṇaṁ vraja*. But if you artificially want to be the predominator, then immediately Kṛṣṇa's illusory energy (*māyā*) is there to entrap you.

We should know that this inclination to be the enjoyer and predominator is the cause of our bondage within this material world. We should know that we are spirit (*ahaṁ brahmāsmi*), without birth or death. Then we should ask, "If as spirit I do not take birth or die, why am I subjected to the sufferings of this material world, such as birth and death? Why have I been put into this condition?" That is intelligence. We are not meant to be conditioned, because we are part and parcel of Kṛṣṇa. Kṛṣṇa is free of all conditioning, and in our natural state we are also free. We may be very small particles of Kṛṣṇa, but just as a gold particle has all the qualities of the mass of gold in the gold mine, so we have all of Kṛṣṇa's qualities in minute degree. We can acquire knowledge of all these things when we follow the instruction of the *Vedānta-*

sūtra: athāto brahma-jijñāsā. "Now therefore, one should inquire into the Absolute Truth."

Unless one inquires into the Absolute Truth and learns how to make a complete solution to the problems of life, one's life is no better than an animal's. In other words, if one remains satisfied in a miserable condition of life, then he is nothing but an animal. Animals cannot understand why they're suffering. When animals are being taken to the slaughterhouse, if one animal enters the slaughterhouse, then every animal will enter easily. They do not understand that they are entering to be slaughtered. This is illusion.

So, here Lord Ṛṣabhadeva is teaching that sex is the cause of the greatest illusion for human beings. Therefore traditional Vedic education taught young boys the value of celibacy, *brahmacarya:* "Don't become entangled with sex life. It is not good. Better to remain celibate. You will be happy." But if one is unable to remain celibate, one may take a wife and live as a gentleman, a regulated householder, or *gṛhastha,* not like cats and dogs. A life of unrestricted sex is not human civilization.

There are many rules and regulations for *gṛhastha* life. *Gṛhastha* life does not permit you to have sex whenever you like. No – once in a month, when conception is most likely; and if the wife is pregnant, then no more sex. That is *gṛhastha* life. Not that a man and woman simply unite and live like animals. That is not *gṛhastha* life but *gṛhamedhī* life. A *gṛhamedhī* is one who does not follow the rules and regulations of married life. He thinks that the pleasure he derives from his wife, children, and home is everything. But a genuine *gṛhastha* is as good as a *sannyāsī* (renunciant). That is why a householder who follows the regulative principles is said to be in the *gṛhastha-āśrama*. An *āśrama* is a place where spiritual life is cultivated. What is the difference between the *gṛhastha-āśrama* and an ordinary home? In an ordinary home one does not follow any regulative principles because one's only purpose is to enjoy sex, family life, and so on, but in the *gṛhastha-āśrama* one leads a regulated life because one's real purpose is self-realization, the development of Kṛṣṇa consciousness.

So as far as possible we should avoid entanglement in sex life. This avoidance is real austerity (*tapasya*). Lord Ṛṣabhadeva began his instructions by recommending austerity: *tapo divyaṁ putrakā yena sattvam śuddhyet*. "O my sons, perform transcendental austerity, by which your existence will be purified." Such austerity begins with celibacy (*tapasā brahmacaryeṇa*). But Kṛṣṇa consciousness is so nice that if one accepts its principles very seriously, then anyone – man or woman, married or unmarried – can remain very happy with Kṛṣṇa as one's lover. In this way, as we advance in Kṛṣṇa consciousness, we can save ourselves from the galaxy of illusion known as this material world, in which there is simply suffering after suffering after suffering.

Chapter Nine

Untie the Knot of Attachment

yadā mano-hṛdaya-granthir asya
karmānubaddho dṛḍha āślatheta
tadā janaḥ samparivartate 'smād
muktaḥ paraṁ yāty atihāya hetum

"When the strong knot in the heart of a person implicated in material life due to the results of past action is slackened, one turns away from his attachment to home, wife, and children. In this way, one gives up the basic principle of illusion [I and mine] and becomes liberated. Thus one goes to the transcendental world."

Śrīmad-Bhāgavatam 5.5.9

When, by associating with *sādhus* and engaging in devotional service, one is gradually freed from the material conception due to knowledge, practice, and detachment, the knot of attachment in the heart is slackened. Thus one can get freed from conditional life and become eligible to return home, back to Godhead.

Here Lord Ṛṣabhadeva is describing the process of liberation. Liberation means no more material life, and the basic principle of material life is sex. Therefore Vedic civilization is based on training people how to become free from sex desire. The great emperor Yāmunācārya described his own experience in this regard:

yad-avadhi mama cetaḥ kṛṣṇa-pādāravinde
nava-nava-rasa-dhāmany udyataṁ rantum āsīt
tad-avadhi bata nārī-saṅgame smaryamāṇe
bhavati mukha-vikāraḥ suṣṭhu niṣṭhīvanaṁ ca

"Ever since I have given my mind and heart to the loving service of the lotus feet of Lord Kṛṣṇa, I have increased my transcendental, blissful life by rendering such service, and thus when I happen to think of sex life, I consider it so abominable that I spit at the thought." This kind of distaste for sex is a sign of the advancement in Kṛṣṇa conscious life.

The four pillars of degradation are illicit sex, meat-eating, intoxication, and gambling. Therefore we forbid our students to indulge in these practices. If you want to make progress in Kṛṣṇa consciousness, you must give these up. When Śrī Caitanya Mahāprabhu delivered Jagāi and Mādhāi, who were addicted to all these practices, the Lord made this condition: "If you promise to give up these four principles of sinful life, I will accept you. Never mind what you have done in the past. Every man is sinful, more or less; there is no doubt about it. That is not a disqualification. But if you agree to give them up now, then immediately you are liberated." Liberation is not very difficult. You can obtain it in a minute, provided you want to take it. Kṛṣṇa promises this in the *Bhagavad-gītā* (18.66):

sarva-dharmān parityajya
mām ekaṁ śaraṇaṁ vraja
ahaṁ tvāṁ sarva-pāpebhyo
mokṣayiṣyāmi mā śucaḥ

"Abandon all varieties of religion and just surrender unto Me. I shall deliver you from all sinful reactions. Do not fear." If you are free from the reactions of sinful life, you are liberated. In other words, you are liberated if you get shelter at the lotus feet of Kṛṣṇa and do not act in such a way that you again fall down into sin. The *Śrīmad-Bhāgavatam* defines liberation as *hitvānyathā-rūpaṁ sva-rūpeṇa vyavasthitiḥ* – giving up our false identification with our gross and subtle bodies and being situated in our *svarūpa*. *Svarūpa* means our original, constitutional position. Lord Caitanya explains: *jīvera 'svarūpa' haya kṛṣṇera 'nitya-dāsa'*: "The constitutional position of the living entity is to be an eternal servant of Kṛṣṇa." As soon as we place ourselves in our original, constitutional position, we are liberated.

Kṛṣṇa describes our constitutional position very simply in the *Bhagavad-gītā* (18.66): *man-manā bhava mad-bhaktaḥ*. "Always think of Me and be ready to serve Me. That's all." The word *bhakta* (devotee) implies *bhakti* ("devotional service") and Bhagavān, the Supreme Personality of Godhead. So, when one engages in devotional service to the Supreme Personality of Godhead,

Lord Kṛṣṇa, one is situated in one's constitutional position and is liberated. This means the hard knot of attachment in the heart is slackened.

One has to understand that he is becoming more and more entangled by material attachments, beginning with sex desire, and that these attachments are engaging him more and more in fruitive activity. When we understand this and try to get free from this business, we become eligible for going back home, back to Godhead. Here Ṛṣabhadeva uses the word *samparivartate,* meaning one has to turn away from the cause of bondage – sex, wife, home, etc. – and turn back toward Kṛṣṇa. That is liberation.

His Divine Grace A. C. Bhaktivedanta Swami Prabhupāda

Founder-*Ācārya* of the International Society for Krishna Consciousness and greatest exponent of Kṛṣṇa consciousness in the modern world.

Those who want to renounce their materialistic pursuits should avoid associating with materialists. Instead they should spend time learning from great souls who have taken shelter of God's spiritual energy and serve the Supreme under their direction. In former ages, one had to seek such persons in the Himalayas or the forest, since they did not live among materialists. (p. 15)

The *Bhagavad-gītā* tells us that humble sages, having true knowledge, see all beings with equal vision and are therefore equally disposed to everyone because they see God, the Supersoul, present in every living entity. They don't think, "He is my countryman, so I shall be kind to him," or "This is an animal, so I shall be kind to it." Rather, they are simply kind to all beings. (p. 16)

Human beings must act differently from animals. Human beings who try to enjoy themselves by eating, drinking, having sex, and sleeping like animals or even plants will be awarded the body of an animal or plant in the next life.

Unless we inquire into the Absolute Truth, beginning with inquiring into who we are and what our purpose is, our lives are no better than an animal's. Animal consciousness means being satisfied with a life of pain. We should use our human form of life for higher consciousness. (p. 2)

We are not the body but the eternal soul within the body. We pass from birth through childhood, adulthood, old age, and death – then repeat this cycle as we move into another body according to the activities we performed in this life. (pp. 20–21)

In the *Bhagavad-gītā* Kṛṣṇa explains that millions of years earlier He had taught the sun god the same yoga science He was now teaching to Arjuna. It's not that because so much time has passed the instructions need updating. The absolute truth is absolute and timeless. (pp. 70–71)

Real civilization means gradually coming to the platform of freeing ourselves from our material absorption and learning to love God, Kṛṣṇa. Real love means that we see our beloved everywhere and in everything. Material loves don't last, and yet our propensity to love fully is innate. When we learn to concentrate our love on Kṛṣṇa, we'll attain the highest perfection of life. (p. 38)

Chapter Ten

The Path to the Highest Pleasure

haṁse gurau mayi bhaktyānuvṛtyā
vitṛṣṇayā dvandva-titikṣayā ca
sarvatra jantor vyasanāvagatyā
jijñāsayā tapasehā-nivṛttyā

mat-karmabhir mat-kathayā ca nityaṁ
mad-deva-saṅgād guṇa-kīrtanān me
nirvaira-sāmyopaśamena putrā
jihāsayā deha-gehātma-buddheḥ

adhyātma-yogena vivikta-sevayā
prāṇendriyātmābhijayena sadhryak
sac-chraddhayā brahmacaryeṇa śaśvad
asampramādena yamena vācām

sarvatra mad-bhāva-vicakṣaṇena
jñānena vijñāna-virājitena
yogena dhṛty-udyama-sattva-yukto
liṅgaṁ vyapohet kuśalo 'ham-ākhyam

"O My sons, you should accept a highly elevated *parama-haṁsa,* a spiritually advanced spiritual master. In this way, you should place your faith and love in Me, the Supreme Personality of Godhead. You should detest sense gratification and tolerate the duality of pleasure and pain, which are like the seasonal changes of summer and winter. Try to realize the miserable condition of living entities, who are miserable even in the higher planetary systems. Philosophically inquire about the truth. Then undergo all kinds of austerities and penances for the sake of devotional service. Give up the endeavor for sense enjoyment and engage in the service of the Lord. Listen to discussions about the Supreme Personality of Godhead, and always associate with devotees. Chant about and glorify the Supreme Lord, and look upon everyone equally on the spiritual platform. Give up enmity and subdue anger and lamentation. Abandon identifying the self with the body and the home, and practice reading the revealed scriptures. Live in a secluded place and practice the process by which you can completely control your life air, mind, and senses. Have full faith in the revealed scriptures, the Vedic literatures, and always observe celibacy. Perform your prescribed duties and avoid unnecessary talks. Always thinking of the Supreme Personality of Godhead, acquire knowledge from the right source. Thus practicing *bhakti-yoga,* you will patiently and enthusiastically be elevated in knowledge and will be able to give up the false ego."

Śrīmad-Bhāgavatam 5.5.10–13

In these four verses, Ṛṣabhadeva tells His sons how they can become free from false ego in material, conditioned life. One gradually becomes liberated by practicing as mentioned above. All these prescribed methods enable one to give up the material body (*liṅgaṁ vyapohet*) and be situated in his original spiritual body. First of all one has to accept a bona fide spiritual master. This is advocated by Śrīla Rūpa Gosvāmī in his *Bhakti-rasāmṛta-sindhu: śrī-guru-pādāśrayaḥ*. To be freed from the entanglement of the material world, one has to approach a spiritual master. *Tad-vijñānārthaṁ sa gurum evābhigacchet* (*Muṇḍaka Upaniṣad* 1.2.12). By questioning the spiritual master and by serving him, one can advance in spiritual life. When one engages in devotional service, naturally the attraction for personal comfort – for eating, sleeping, and dressing – is reduced. When one associates with devotees, a spiritual standard is maintained. The word *mad-deva-saṅgāt* ("association with My devotees") is very important. There are many so-called religions devoted to the worship of various demigods, but here good association means association with one who simply accepts Kṛṣṇa as his worshipable Deity.

Another important item is *dvandva-titikṣā* ("tolerance of material dualities"). As long as one is situated in the material world, there must be pleasure and pain arising from the material body. As Kṛṣṇa advises in the *Bhagavad-gītā, tāṁs titikṣava bhārata*. One has to learn how to tolerate the temporary pains and pleasures of this material world. One must also be detached from his family and practice celibacy. Sex with one's wife according to the scriptural injunctions is also accepted as *brahmacarya* (celibacy), but illicit sex is opposed to religious principles, and it hampers advancement in spiritual consciousness. Another important word is *vijñāna-virājita*. Everything should be done very scientifically and consciously. One should be a realized soul. In this way, one can give up the entanglement of material bondage.

As Śrī Madhvācārya points out, the sum and substance of these four *ślokas* is that one should refrain from acting out of a desire for sense gratification and should instead always engage in the Lord's loving service. In other words, *bhakti-yoga* is the acknowledged path of liberation. Śrīla Madhvācārya quotes from the *Adhyātma:*

ātmano 'vihitaṁ karma
varjayitvānya-karmaṇaḥ
kāmasya ca parityāgo
nirīhety āhur uttamāḥ

One should perform activities only for the benefit of the soul; any other activity should be given up. When a person is situated in this way, he is said to be desireless. Actually a living entity cannot be totally desireless, but when he desires the benefit the soul and nothing else, he is said to be desireless.

Spiritual knowledge is *jñāna-vijñāna-samanvitam*. And when one is fully equipped with *jñāna* and *vijñāna,* he is perfect. *Jñāna* means that one understands the Supreme

Personality of Godhead, Viṣṇu, to be the Supreme Being. *Vijñāna* refers to the activities that liberate one from the ignorance of material existence. As stated in *Śrīmad-Bhāgavatam* (2.9.31): *jñānaṁ parama-guhyaṁ me yad vijñāna-samanvitam.* Knowledge of the Supreme Lord is very confidential, and the supreme knowledge by which one understands Him further the liberation of all living entities. This knowledge is *vijñāna*. As Lord Kṛṣṇa confirms in the *Bhagavad-gītā* (4.9):

janma karma ca me divyam
evaṁ yo vetti tattvataḥ
tyaktvā dehaṁ punar janma
naiti mām eti so 'rjuna

"One who knows the transcendental nature of My appearance and activities does not, upon leaving the body, take his birth again in this material world, but attains My eternal abode, O Arjuna."

In text 9, Lord Ṛṣabhadeva recommended that one slacken the knots of attachment in the heart, and the items listed in these verses are the means by which one can do this. Unfortunately, in the modern world almost everyone is busy from morning till late at night increasing those attachments. Working in big, big factories day and night, one shift after another – this unnecessarily severe hard work (*ugra-karma*) has become a most conspicuous feature of modern civilization. We have seen such *ugra-karma* in Detroit. In the assembly plants where they manufacture Ford motorcars, one man is simply putting on the wheels of the motorcar. He has a huge stock of wheels nearby. And somebody else is putting on the tires. He has a huge stock of tires. There are so many motorcar parts – three thousand parts. So there are big, big factories elsewhere where men are working day and night to manufacture the different parts of the motorcar. And ultimately the parts are sent to the factory in Detroit where they assemble one car after another, and people are using a huge quantity of cars. After working day and night in the factories, people try to pacify themselves by intoxication and illicit sex. All this *ugra-karma* keeps one bound up by unlimited material attachments.

Despite all this *ugra-karma,* however, people are not happy. They do not know that happiness cannot be had with *ugra-karma*. Therefore here Lord Ṛṣabhadeva says that one of the principles of advancement is *sarvatra jantor vyasanāvagatyā,* seeing that in the material world there is misery everywhere, even on higher planets. As Kṛṣṇa says in the *Bhagavad-gītā, ā-brahma-bhuvanāl lokāḥ punar āvartino 'rjuna:* "From the highest planet down to the lowest, all are places of misery." And also *duḥkhālayam aśāśvatam:* "This material world is a place of misery where life is temporary."

So, we should know that although we are trying to improve our material condition in so many ways, it is ultimately impossible to do so. If a poor man works very hard and acquires a great amount of wealth, that does not mean he is free from the dangerous conditions of life, because the threefold miseries are present everywhere. These are miseries pertaining to the body and mind, miseries caused by other living entities, and miseries brought on by the forces of nature. And of course there are always the miseries of birth, old age, disease, and death.

All these miseries are caused by the material body, whose root is the false ego. This false ego can be given up if we take up the practices Lord Ṛṣabhadeva describes here: *liṅgaṁ vyapohet kuśalo 'jam-ākhyam*. The first practice is surrendering to a highly advanced spiritual master (*haṁse gurau mayi bhaktyānuvṛtyā*). This is the beginning of real religion. If you do not get a qualified guru, then everything is bogus. But if by good fortune you get the association of a qualified guru, then you can receive the seed of the creeper of devotion. As Lord Caitanya says, *guru-kṛṣṇa-prasāde pāya bhakti-latā-bīja:* "By the mercy of both the spiritual master and Kṛṣṇa, the fortunate soul receives within his heart the seed of the creeper of devotion." Therefore here Ṛṣabhadeva, who is an incarnation of Kṛṣṇa, says *haṁse gurau mayi bhaktyānuvṛtyā:* "One must render devotional service first to the spiritual master and then to Me." You cannot jump over the spiritual master and go to Kṛṣṇa. Some rascals say, "Well, I know Kṛṣṇa. I shall go to Kṛṣṇa directly, without a guru." No, that is not possible. First of all guru, then Kṛṣṇa. And if one actually follows the instructions given by the guru and the scriptures, then one's strong desire to enjoy this material world will be slackened and one's liberation from material miseries is assured.

Chapter Eleven

Attaining All Perfection

karmāśayaṁ hṛdaya-granthi-bandham
avidyayāsāditam apramattaḥ
anena yogena yathopadeśaṁ
samyag vyapohyoparameta yogāt

"As I have advised you, My dear sons, you should act accordingly. Be very careful. By these means you will be freed from the ignorance of the desire for fruitive activity, and the knot of bondage in the heart will be completely severed. For further advancement, you should also give up the means. That is, you should not become attached to the process of liberation itself."

Śrīmad-Bhāgavatam 5.5.14

The process of liberation is *brahma-jijñāsā,* the search for the Absolute Truth. Generally, *brahma-jijñāsā* is called *neti neti,* the process by which one analyzes existence to search out the Absolute Truth. This method continues as long as one is not situated in his spiritual life. Spiritual life is *brahma-bhūta,* the self-realized state. In the words of the *Bhagavad-gītā* (18.54):

brahma-bhūtaḥ prasannātmā
na śocati na kāṅkṣati
samaḥ sarveṣu bhūteṣu
mad-bhaktiṁ labhate parām

"One who is thus transcendentally situated at once realizes the Supreme Brahman and becomes fully joyful. He never laments nor desires to have anything; he is equally disposed to every living entity. In that state, he attains pure devotional service unto Me."

The idea is to enter into the *parā bhakti,* the transcendental devotional service of the Supreme Lord. To attain this, one must analyze one's existence, but when one is actually engaged in devotional service he should not bother seeking out knowledge. By simply engaging in devotional service undeviatingly, one will always remain in the liberated condition. *Bhagavad-gītā* (14.26) states:

māṁ ca yo 'vyabhicāreṇa
bhakti-yogena sevate
sa guṇān samatītyaitān
brahma-bhūyāya kalpate

The unflinching execution of devotional service automatically places one on the transcendental platform, called the *brahma-bhūta* stage. Another important feature in this connection is *anena yogena yathopadeśam*. The instructions received from the spiritual master must be followed immediately. One should not deviate from or surpass the instructions of the spiritual master. One should not be simply intent on consulting books but should simultaneously execute the spiritual master's order (*yathopadeśam*). Mystic power should be achieved to enable one to give up the material conception, but when one actually engages in devotional service, one does not need to practice the mystic yoga system. The point is that one can give up the practice of yoga, but devotional service cannot be given up. As stated in the *Śrīmad-Bhāgavatam* (1.7.10):

ātmārāmāś ca munayo
nirgranthā apy urukrame
kurvanty ahaitukīṁ bhaktim
ittham-bhūta-guṇo hariḥ

Even those who are liberated [*ātmārāma*] must always engage in devotional service. One may give up the practice of yoga when one is self-realized, but at no stage can one give up devotional service. All other activities for self-realization, including yoga and philosophical speculation, may be given up, but devotional service must be retained at all times.

Devotional service will free us from *karmāśayam,* the desire for fruitive activity. As long as our mind is absorbed in fruitive activity, there is no question of becoming free from bondage to the material body (*karmātmakaṁ yena śarīra-bandhaḥ*). The whole purpose of human life is to free the spirit soul from bondage to the body and thus from the suffering caused by the repetition of birth and death. Everyone is trying to become happy by working hard and enjoying the results – not only here on earth but also on other planets, even up to the highest planet, Brahmaloka. But this process simply increases our bondage to the material body. In texts 10 through 13, Lord Ṛṣabhadeva explained the process of devotional service, by which one can gradually become free from this bondage.

Devotional service is a science; it is not sentiment. Therefore we have to understand it from authorized sources of Vedic knowledge. Such knowledge is not based on our imperfect senses, and so in the Vedic knowledge there is no mistake, cheating, or illusion. Everything is perfect. This is real science – perfect knowledge. Not "perhaps," "it may be" – that is not science but theory.

To know the science of devotional service, one has to approach a perfect teacher (*tad vijñānārthaṁ sa gurum evābhigacchet*). In text 10 Lord Ṛṣabhadeva confirms that the first step in devotional service is *haṁse gurau mayi bhaktyānuvṛtyā:* "One should surrender to a highly elevated spiritual master and in this way render devotional service to Me, the Supreme Personality of Godhead." The word *mayi,* "unto Me, the Supreme Personality of Godhead," is significant. This indicates that the guru is as good as the Supreme Lord because he does not deviate from the instructions of the Lord. That is the primary characteristic of the guru: he does not manufacture something new. No, he teaches the same thing that Kṛṣṇa taught five thousand years ago in the *Bhagavad-gītā*. And even when Kṛṣṇa spoke it then it was not new. In the fourth chapter of the *Bhagavad-gītā* (4.1) Kṛṣṇa says to Arjuna, *sa evāyaṁ mayā te 'dya yogaḥ proktaḥ purātanaḥ:* "The same science of yoga I taught to the sun god millions of years ago today I am teaching to you." It is not that because time has passed that the instruction must be changed. This is nonsense. There cannot be something new in the matter of the science of the Absolute Truth. Everything is established. Millions of years ago the sun rose on the eastern horizon, and still it is rising in the east. It is not that now the sun is rising on the western or northern horizon. Similarly, Vedic knowledge is eternally established. It cannot be changed under any circumstance. What was true millions of years ago is still true now. And to know that truth, one has to approach a bona fide spiritual master.

Two of the most important steps in devotional service given by Lord Ṛṣabhadeva are *mat-karmabhiḥ,* "working for Me," and *mat-kathayā ca nityam,* "always hearing and chanting about Me." The word *nityam,* "always," is very important here. One should not attend classes in *Śrīmad-Bhāgavatam* for seven or ten days a year and the other 355 days go to the stock market and simply inquire about the price of this share or that share. No, you have to hear the *Bhāgavatam* daily in the association of devotees (*mad-deva saṅgāt*), not in the association of fruitive workers or mental speculators. That will not help us.

Another important item in devotional service is *jihāsayā deha-gehātma-buddheḥ:* by executing devotional service one should develop detachment from family life. *Bhāgavatam* 11.2.42 states, *bhaktiḥ pareśānubhavo viraktir anyatra ca:* "By the practice of *bhakti-yoga* one feels the transcendental pleasure of serving the Lord, experiences

His presence, and feels detachment from everything else." That is *bhakti-yoga*. Everyone can test his progress on the path of devotional service by asking himself, "How much have I become detached from worldly affection? How much am I still thinking 'This is my body, this is my country, this is my society, this is my wife, these are my children'?" We have to give up these illusory attachments. If we are not able to give up worldly attachment, then we cannot make any progress. One has to come to understand *ahaṁ brahmāsmi:* "I am not this body, I am not this mind, I am not this intelligence. I am pure spirit [*brahman*], part and parcel of Kṛṣṇa, the Supreme Brahman."

If we practice devotional service according to the instructions given here in the *Bhāgavatam* and in other bona fide scriptures (*śāstras*), we will be successful and become liberated. But without scripture, it is not possible. As Kṛṣṇa says in the *Bhagavad-gītā* (16.23), *yaḥ śāstra-vidhim utsṛjya vartate kāma kārataḥ na sa siddhim avāpnoti:* "If you give up the instructions of scripture and act according to your whims, then there is no question of perfection." And Rūpa Gosvāmī confirms this in his *Bhakti-rasāmṛta-sindhu* (1.2.101):

śruti-smṛti-purāṇādi-
pañcarātra-vidhiṁ vinā
aikāntikī harer bhaktir
utpātāyaiva kalpate

"Devotional service of the Lord that ignores the authorized Vedic literatures like the *Upaniṣads, Purāṇas,* and *Nārada Pañcarātra* is simply an unnecessary disturbance in society." There are so many religious practices that have been invented. For example, the scriptures prescribe the chanting of the Hare Kṛṣṇa mantra, but people have invented so many ways of chanting. If you chant Rāma, Rāma, Rāma, Rādhe Rādhe Rādhe, Kṛṣṇa, Kṛṣṇa, Kṛṣṇa, that is also chanting the holy name, but you have to follow the scripture. The scripture says chant Hare Kṛṣṇa Hare Kṛṣṇa, Kṛṣṇa Kṛṣṇa Hare Hare / Hare Rāma Hare Rāma, Rāma Rāma Hare Hare. You have to accept that. Not that you chant *nitāi-gaura rādhe-śyāma, hare kṛṣṇa hare rāma*. No. What is the value of your invention? You are not perfect. You cannot invent a new mantra and be successful. Simply follow the recommendations of scripture and you will attain all perfection.

Appendices

The Author

His Divine Grace A.C. Bhaktivedanta Swami Prabhupāda appeared in this world in 1896 in Calcutta, India. He first met his spiritual master, Śrīla Bhaktisiddhānta Sarasvatī Gosvāmī, in Calcutta in 1922. Bhaktisiddhānta Sarasvatī, a prominent religious scholar and the founder of sixty-four Gauḍīya Maṭhas (Vedic institutes), liked this educated young man and convinced him to dedicate his life to teaching Vedic knowledge. Śrīla Prabhupāda became his student and, in 1933, his formally initiated disciple.

At their first meeting, in 1922, Śrīla Bhaktisiddhānta Sarasvatī requested Śrīla Prabhupāda to broadcast Vedic knowledge in English. In the years that followed, Śrīla Prabhupāda wrote a commentary on the *Bhagavad-gītā,* assisted the Gauḍīya Maṭha in its work and, in 1944, started *Back to Godhead,* an English fortnightly magazine. Singlehandedly, Śrīla Prabhupāda edited it, typed the manuscripts, checked the galley proofs, and even distributed the individual copies. The magazine is now being continued by his disciples.

In 1950 Śrīla Prabhupāda retired from married life, adopting the *vānaprastha* (retired) order to devote more time to his studies and writing. He traveled to the holy city of Vṛndāvana, where he lived in humble circumstances in the historic temple of Rādhā-Dāmodara. There he engaged for several years in deep study and writing. He accepted the renounced order of life (*sannyāsa*) in 1959. At Rādhā-Dāmodara, Śrīla Prabhupāda began work on his life's masterpiece: a multivolume commentated translation of the eighteen-thousand-verse *Śrīmad-Bhāgavatam* (*Bhāgavata Purāṇa*). He also wrote *Easy Journey to Other Planets.*

After publishing three volumes of the *Bhāgavatam,* Śrīla Prabhupāda came to the United States, in September 1965, to fulfill the mission of his spiritual master. Subsequently, His Divine Grace wrote more than fifty volumes of authoritative commentated translations and summary studies of the philosophical and religious classics of India.

When he first arrived by freighter in New York City, Śrīla Prabhupāda was practically penniless. Only after almost a year of great difficulty did he establish the International Society for Krishna Consciousness, in July of 1966. Before he passed away on November 14, 1977, he had guided the Society and seen it grow to a worldwide confederation of more than one hundred *āśramas,* schools, temples, institutes, and farm communities. New centers continue to open worldwide.

In 1972 His Divine Grace introduced the Vedic system of primary and secondary education in the West by founding the *gurukula* school in Dallas, Texas. Since then his disciples have established similar schools throughout the United States and the rest of the world.

Śrīla Prabhupāda also inspired the construction of

several large international cultural centers in India. At Śrīdhāma Māyāpur, in West Bengal, devotees are building a spiritual city centered on a magnificent temple – an ambitious project for which construction will extend over many years to come. In Vṛndāvana are the Krishna-Balaram Temple and International Guesthouse, *gurukula* school, and Śrīla Prabhupāda Memorial and Museum. There are also major temples and cultural centers in Mumbai, New Delhi, Ahmedabad, Siliguri, and Ujjain. Other centers are planned in many important locations on the Indian subcontinent and around the world.

Śrīla Prabhupāda's most significant contribution, however, is his books. Highly respected by scholars for their authority, depth, and clarity, they have been used as textbooks in numerous college courses. His writings have been translated into over a hundred languages. The Bhaktivedanta Book Trust, established in 1972 to publish the works of His Divine Grace, has thus become the world's largest publisher of books in the field of Indian religion and philosophy.

In just twelve years, despite his advanced age, Śrīla Prabhupāda circled the globe fourteen times on lecture tours that took him to six continents. In spite of such a vigorous schedule, Śrīla Prabhupāda continued to write prolifically. His writings constitute a veritable library of Vedic philosophy, religion, literature, and culture.

Glossary

Absolute Truth – the ultimate source of all energies.

Arjuna – one of the five Pāṇḍava brothers. Kṛṣṇa became his chariot driver and spoke the *Bhagavad-gītā* to him.

Bhagavad-gītā – a seven-hundred-verse record of a conversation between Lord Kṛṣṇa and His disciple Arjuna, recorded in the *Mahābhārata.*

Bhakti-yoga – the system of cultivation of *bhakti,* or pure devotional service to God, which is untinged by sense gratification or philosophical speculation.

Brahmā – the first created being and secondary creator of the material universe.

Brahman – the impersonal, all-pervasive aspect of the Supreme.

Brāhmaṇa – a member of the intellectual, priestly class.

Caitanya-caritāmṛta – the foremost biography of Śrī Caitanya Mahāprabhu, written in the sixteenth century by Śrīla Kṛṣṇadāsa Kavirāja Gosvāmī.

Caitanya Mahāprabhu (1486–1534) – Lord Kṛṣṇa in the aspect of His own devotee.

Demigods – universal controllers and residents of the higher material planets.

False ego – the conception that "I am the material body, mind, or intelligence."

Gopīs – Kṛṣṇa's cowherd girlfriends and His most surrendered and confidential devotees.

Guru – spiritual master.

Impersonalist – one who adheres to the philosophy that everything is one and that the Absolute Truth is not a person.

Jñāna – knowledge.

Jñānī – one engaged in the cultivation of knowledge, especially through philosophical speculation.

Karma – any material action that will incur a subsequent reaction.

Karmīs – fruitive actors.

Kṛṣṇa – the Supreme Personality of Godhead and origin of all expansions.

Madhvācārya – a great devotee scholar and teacher who lived in India during the thirteenth century.

Mahātmā – lit., "great soul." One who understands that Kṛṣṇa is everything and who therefore surrenders to Him.

Mantra – a transcendental sound vibration or a Vedic hymn.

Nārada Pañcarātra – Nārada Muni's text on the process of Deity worship and mantra meditation.

Narottama dāsa Ṭhākura – a renowned sixteenth-century Vaiṣṇava in the disciplic succession from Śrī Caitanya Mahāprabhu who is famous for his writing of devotional songs.

Padma Purāṇa – one of the eighteen *Purāṇas*.

Parabrahman – the Supreme Personality of Godhead, Śrī Kṛṣṇa.

Prahlāda Mahārāja – a great devotee of Lord Kṛṣṇa who was persecuted by his atheistic father, Hiraṇyakaśipu, but who was protected by the Lord.

Purāṇas – historical supplements to the *Vedas*.

Ṛṣabhadeva – an incarnation of the Supreme Lord as a devotee king who, after instructing His sons in spiritual life, renounced His kingdom for a life of austerity.

Rūpa Gosvāmī – chief of the Six Gosvāmīs of Vṛndāvana, who were empowered by Śrī Caitanya Mahāprabhu to establish and distribute the philosophy of Kṛṣṇa consciousness.

Sannyāsī – a renunciant.

Śloka – a Sanskrit verse.

Śrīmad-Bhāgavatam – the foremost of the eighteen *Purāṇas*. The complete science of God, it establishes the supreme position of Lord Kṛṣṇa.

Supersoul – the localized aspect of the Supreme Lord living in the heart of each living entity.

Upaniṣad – a Sanskrit treatise that embodies the philosophy of the *Vedas*.

Vaiṣṇava – a devotee of Viṣṇu, or Kṛṣṇa.

Varṇāśrama-dharma – the system of the four social and four spiritual orders of a Vedic society.

Vasudeva – the Supreme Lord, Kṛṣṇa.

Vedānta-sūtra – Śrīla Vyāsadeva's conclusive summary of Vedic knowledge, written in aphorisms.

Vedas – the four original scriptures: *Ṛg, Sāma, Atharva,* and *Yajur*.

Vijñāna – practical realization of spiritual knowledge.

Vṛndāvana – Kṛṣṇa's eternal abode; the village on this earth where He enacted His childhood pastimes.

Sanskrit Pronunciation Guide

The system of transliteration used in this book conforms to a system that scholars have accepted to indicate the pronunciation of each sound in the Sanskrit language.

The short vowel **a** is pronounced like the **u** in b**u**t, long **ā** like the **a** in f**a**r. Short **i** is pronounced as **i** in p**i**n, long **ī** as in p**i**que, short **u** as in p**u**ll, and long **ū** as in r**u**le. The vowel **ṛ** is pronounced like **ri** in **ri**m, **e** like the **ey** in th**ey**, **o** like the **o** in g**o**, **ai** like the **ai** in **ai**sle, and **au** like the **ow** in h**ow**. The *anusvara* (**ṁ**) is pronounced like the **n** in the French word *bon*, and *visarga* (**ḥ**) is pronounced as a final **h** sound. At the end of a couplet, **aḥ** is pronounced **aha**, and **iḥ** is pronounced **ihi**.

The guttural consonants – **k**, **kh**, **g**, **gh** and **ṅ** – are pronounced from the throat in much the same manner as in English. **K** is pronounced as in **k**ite, **kh** as in Ec**kh**art, **g** as in **g**ive, **gh** as in di**g-h**ard, and **ṅ** as in si**ng**.

The palatal consonants – **c**, **ch**, **j**, **jh** and **ñ** – are pronounced with the tongue touching the firm ridge behind the teeth. **C** is pronounced as in **ch**air, **ch** as in staun**ch-h**eart, **j** as in **j**oy, **jh** as in he**dgeh**og, and **ñ** as in ca**ny**on.

The cerebral consonants – **ṭ**, **ṭh**, **ḍ**, **ḍh** and **ṇ** – are pronounced with the tip of the tongue turned up and drawn back against the dome of the palate. **Ṭ** is pronounced as in **t**ub, **ṭh** as in ligh**t-h**eart, **ḍ** as in **d**ove, **ḍh** as in re**d-h**ot, and **ṇ** as in **n**ut.

The dental consonants – **t, th, d, dh** and **n** – are pronounced in the same manner as the cerebrals, but with the forepart of the tongue against the teeth.

The labial consonants – **p, ph, b, bh** and **m** – are pronounced with the lips. **P** is pronounced as in **p**ine, **ph** as in u**ph**ill, **b** as in **b**ird, **bh** as in ru**b-h**ard, and **m** as in **m**other.

The semivowels – **y, r, l** and **v** – are pronounced as in **y**es, **r**un, **l**ight and **v**ine respectively. The sibilants – **ś, ṣ** and **s** – are pronounced, respectively, as in the German word *sprechen* and the English words **sh**ine and **s**un. The letter **h** is pronounced as in **h**ome.

International Society for Krishna Consciousness

Founder-*Ācārya:* His Divine Grace A.C. Bhaktivedanta Swami Prabhupāda

More addresses on **directory.krishna.com** and **centres.iskcon.org**.

✦ center with restaurant

Australia, Sydney – 180 Falcon Street, North Sydney, NSW 2060; +61 2 9959 4558; info@iskcon.com.au; iskcon.com.au

Belgium, Durbuy ✦ Domaine de Radhadesh, Petite Somme 5, 6940 Durbuy; +32 86 32 35 90; info@radhadesh.com; radhadesh.com

Bulgaria, Sofia – bul. "Kliment Ohridski" 117, kv. Malinova Dolina, 1756 Sofia; +359 2 961 6050; iskconsofia@gmail.com; krishnabg.com

Canada, Toronto – 243 Avenue Road, Toronto, ON M5R 2J6; +1 416 922-5415; info@torontokrishna.com; torontokrishna.com

Croatia, Zagreb – Ul. Bizek II 36, 10090, Zagreb; +385 91 349 07 02; zagreb@iskcon.hr; zagreb.iskcon.hr

Czech Republic, Prague – Chrám Šrí Šrí Nitái Navadvípačandry, Lužce 48, 267 18 Lužce; +420 311 516 558; chram108@gmail.com; harekrsna.cz

Denmark, Copenhagen – Skjulhøj Allé 44, 2720 Vanløse; +45 48 28 64 46; iskcon.denmark@pamho.net; krishna.dk

England, London (Central) ✦ Sri Sri Radha-Krishna Temple, 10 Soho Street, London, W1D 3DL; +44 20 7437 3662; +44 20 3687 0617; info@iskcon-london.org; govindas@iskcon-london.org; iskcon-london.org

England, Manchester – 20 Mayfield Road, Whalley Range, Manchester, M16 8FT; +44 161 226 4416; contact@iskconmanchester.com; iskconmanchester.com

England, Watford – Bhaktivedanta Manor, Hilfield Lane, Herts, Watford, WD25 8EZ; +44 1923 851000; info@krishnatemple.com; krishnatemple.com

France, Luçay-le-Mâle – La Nouvelle Mayapura, Château d'Oublaisse, 36360 Luçay-le-Mâle; +33 7 83 20 70 04; contact@newmayapur.com; newmayapur.com

France, Paris – 230 Avenue de la Division Leclerc, 95200 Sarcelles; +33 7 83 20 70 04; iskconfr@gmail.com; iskconparis.org

Germany, Abentheuer – Goloka Dhama, Böckingstraße 4a, 55767 Abentheuer; +49 6782 2214; golokadhama.de@gmail.com; goloka-dhama.de

Germany, Berlin – Jagannatha-Tempel, Berliner Allee 209, 13088 Berlin; mail@tempelberlin.de; tempelberlin.de

Germany, Jandelsbrunn – Simhachalam, Zielberg 20, 94118 Jandelsbrunn; +49 8583 316; info@simhachalam.de; simhachalam.de

Hungary, Budapest – Lehel u. 15-17, 1039 Budapest; +36 1 391 04 35; info@krisna.hu; krisna.hu

Hungary, Somogyvámos ✦ Krisna-völgy, Fő u. 38, 8699 Somogyvámos; +36 30 641 2309; +36 6 85 540 002; info@krisnavolgy.hu; krisnavolgy.hu

India, Mayapur ✦ Shree Mayapur Chandrodaya Mandir, District Nadia, Shree Mayapur Dham 741313; +91 9474 751202; mayapur.chandrodaya@pamho.net; mayapur.com

India, Mumbai ✦ Hare Krishna Land, Juhu, Mumbai 400049; +91 22 2620 6860; iskcon.juhu@pamho.net; guesthouse.mumbai@pamho.net; iskconmumbai.com

India, New Delhi ✦ Hare Krishna Hill, Sant Nagar Main Road, East of Kailash, New Delhi 110065; +91 11 2623 5133; info@iskcondelhi.com; iskcondelhi.com

India, Vrindavan ✦ Krishna-Balaram Mandir, Bhaktivedanta Swami Marg, Raman Reti, Mathura, Vrindavan 281121; +91 565 254 0021; info@iskconvrindavan.com; iskconvrindavan.com

Ireland, Dublin ✦ Govinda's Kirtan Centre, 83 Middle Abbey Street, Dublin 1, D01 EV91; +353 86 858 2392; manu@iskcondublin.com; iskcondublin.com

Italy, Florence ✦ Villa Vrindavana, Via Scopeti 108, San Casciano in Val di Pesa, 50026 Firenze FI; +39 055 820054; info@villavrindavana.org; villavrindavana.org

Italy, Rome – Domus Hare Krishna, Via Pratolungo 56, 00049 Velletri RM; +39 328 683 3551; info@harekrsna.it; harekrsna.it

Nepal, Kathmandu – Hare Krishna Dham, Budhanilkantha 5, Kathmandu 44622; +977 980-1205731; info@iskconnepal.org; iskconnepal.org

New Zealand, Auckland – 1229 Coatesville-Riverhead Highway, Kumeū 0892; +64 9 412 8075; facebook.com/nzharekrishna; harekrishna.org.nz

Northern Ireland, Belfast – 2a Brooklands Grange, Dunmurry, Belfast, BT17 0SA; +44 74 2448 3907; info@iskconbelfast.co.uk; facebook.com/Iskconbelfast; iskconbelfast.co.uk

Russia, Moscow ✦ Kuusinena st. 19A, Moscow, 125252; +7 (925) 9971003; info@krishna-temple.ru; krishna-temple.ru

Scotland, Lesmahagow – Karuna Bhavan, Bankhouse Road, Lesmahagow, Lanarkshire, ML11 0ES; +44 7957 647168; info@iskconscotland.org; iskconscotland.org

Slovenia, Ljubljana – Žibertova 27, 1000 Ljubljana; +386 1 431 21 24; hkc.ljubljana@gmail.com; harekrisna.net

South Africa, Durban ✦ 50 Bhaktivedanta Swami Circle, Chatsworth, 4092; +27 31 403 3328; temple@iskcondurban.net; iskcondurban.net

Spain, Barcelona – Pl. Reial, 12, Entresuelo 2º, 08002 Barcelona; +34 933 02 51 94; info@krishnabcn.com; krishnabcn.com

Spain, Tenerife ✦ Vedic Cultural Centre, Rafael Puig Lluvina 32, C.C. Parque Santiago II, 330, 38660 Playa de las Américas; +34 635 172 411; info@iskcontenerife.es; iskcontenerife.es

Sweden, Järna – Almviks Gård, 15395 Järna; +46 8 551 520 50; almviks.gard@pamho.net; almviksgard.se

Sweden, Stockholm – New Radhakunda, Korsnäs Gård, 14792 Grödinge; +46-853029800; info@pamho.net; krishna.se

Switzerland, Langenthal – Gaura Bhaktiyoga Center, Dorfgasse 43, 4900 Langenthal; +41 76 507 04 99; gaura.bhaktiyoga.center@gmx.ch; gaura-bhakti.ch

Switzerland, Zurich – Krishna-Gemeinschaft Schweiz, Bergstrasse 54, 8032 Zürich; +41 44 262 33 88; info@krishna.ch; krishna.ch

Ukraine, Kyiv – Zorany per. 16, Kyiv, 04078; +38 (098) 551 59 53, +38 (063) 645 11 23; krishna.org.ua

USA, Los Angeles ✦ 3764 Watseka Ave., Los Angeles, CA 90034; +1 310 836 2676; jagabeca@gmail.com; jagannivas.la@gmail.com; iskconla.com

USA, Moundsville ✦ New Vrindaban, 3759 McCreary's Ridge Road, Moundsville, WV 26041; +1 304 843 1600; mail@newvrindaban.com; newvrindaban.com

USA, New York City ✦ Bhakti Center, 25 First Avenue, New York City, NY 10003; +1 212 533 4842; hello@bhakticenter.org; bhakticenter.org

Wales, Cardiff – Ty Krishna Cymru, 4 Dock Chambers, Bute Street, Cardiff, CF10 5AG; +44 29 2019 3346; help@tykrishna.cymru; tykrishna.cymru

Bhagavad-gītā As It Is

Translation and commentary by
His Divine Grace A. C. Bhaktivedanta Swami Prabhupāda

A primary resource on yoga and a concise summary of Vedic wisdom, the *Bhagavad-gītā* discusses the nature of consciousness, the meaning of life, karma, the difference between matter and spirit, and what happens after death. *Bhagavad-gītā As It Is* is the largest-selling edition of the *Gītā* in the Western world. Its author, A. C. Bhaktivedanta Swami Prabhupāda, while remaining loyal to the intended meaning of Kṛṣṇa's words, has unlocked the secrets of the *Gītā's* ancient knowledge and invited us, as Kṛṣṇa invites Arjuna, to walk from perplexity to spiritual enlightenment.

Large: Hardbound with dustjacket, 960 pages, 48 color plates, 152 x 228 mm, ISBN 978-91-7769-312-3
Medium: Hardbound, 832 pages, 16 color plates, 125 x 190 mm, ISBN 978-91-7769-316-1
Small: Hardbound, 1024 pages, 16 color plates, 102 x 155 mm, ISBN 978-91-7149-958-5

Print book	Amazon • blservices.com
Ebook	Amazon's Kindle Store • Apple Books Store • Google Play Books
Audiobook	bbtmedia.com
Book app	Apple's App Store • Google Play

Śrī Īśopaniṣad

Translation and commentary by
His Divine Grace A. C. Bhaktivedanta Swami Prabhupāda

Seekers have consulted the 108 mystical *Upaniṣads* for thousands of years. As a key Vedic text, *Śrī Īśopaniṣad,* in just 18 mantras, explores the nature of divinity, the cosmos, and the self. The clear commentary by His Divine Grace A. C. Bhaktivedanta Swami Prabhupāda helps readers navigate the philosophical concepts of the *Īśopaniṣad* and discover the relationship between matter and spirit and their own relationship with the *īśa,* the beautiful Supreme Soul.

Softcover, 144 pages, 8 color plates, 110 x 178 mm
ISBN 978-91-7769-238-6

Print book	Amazon • blservices.com
Ebook	Amazon's Kindle Store • Apple Books Store • Google Play Books
Audiobook	bbtmedia.com